# Exploring and Mapping the American West

## JUDY ALTER

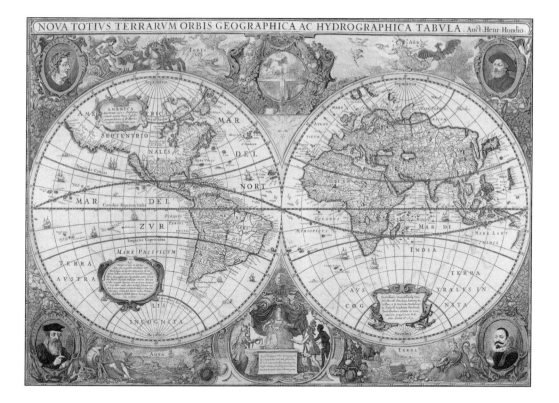

NOVA TOTIVS TERRARVM ORBIS GEOGRAPHICA AC HYDROGRAPHICA TABVLA. Auct Henr Hondio.

New ... ...lney
Danbury, Connecticut

*Reading Consultant:* Linda Cornwell, Coordinator of School Quality
and Professional Improvement Indiana State Teachers Association

Visit Children's Press on the Internet at:
http://publishing.grolier.com

Library of Congress Cataloging-in-Publication Data

Alter, Judy, 1938–
    Exploring and Mapping the American West / Judy Alter.
        p. cm.—(Cornerstones of freedom)
    Includes index.
    Summary: Describes the exploration and mapping of the American
West from prehistoric Indian maps through the geographical
information gathered by the Spanish explorers, the expeditions of
Lewis and Clark and Zebulon Pike, and the mapping done by the U.S.
Army and the railroad companies.
    ISBN 0-516-21599-X (lib. bdg.)   0-516-27279-9 (pbk.)
    1. Cartography—West (U.S.)—History—Juvenile literature. 2. West
(U.S.)—Discovery and exploration—Juvenile literature. 3. West (U.S.)—
Description and travel—Juvenile literature. [1. Cartography—West
(U.S.)—History. 2. West (U.S.)—Maps. 3. West (U.S.)—Discovery and
exploration.] I. Title. II. Series.

GA408.5W47 A57 2001
912.78-dc21
00-023533

For more than ten thousand years, many tribes of American Indians lived in the land west of the Mississippi River—the American West. These peoples were the first to explore this land and make maps of it. Maps helped them show what the land beyond their villages looked like or how to travel from one place to another. Prehistoric Indians sometimes drew maps on rocks or on the walls of caves. These maps are called petroglyphs (Peh-truh-GLIFS).

Some petroglyphs mark ancient travel routes. Early Indian tribes left their maps in spots where others were likely to see them, such as where two trails crossed or in a cave used for shelter. A famous petroglyph called Map Rock is located near what is now Givens Hot Springs, Idaho. Map Rock is large—about the size of a dining room rug. Some historians think early Indians drew a map of the Snake and Salmon Rivers on Map Rock. Petroglyphs and other Indian maps are not like the maps people use today.

*Map Rock is in a field of petroglyphs. Historians think that many American Indians drew petroglyphs here because the Snake River—a water route—is nearby.*

An American Indian might draw a map in the dirt or sand to show another person a good place to hunt. However, that drawing would disappear with a gust of wind, a few drops of rain, or the next footstep. Other Indian maps might be sketched on tree bark or animal hide and left behind for someone else to use, but these maps were not intended to be permanent documents. Most locations were described by word of mouth, not by written documents. American Indians often relayed information through stories that were repeated many times by different people. They told the stories of their maps, perhaps around fires at night, rather than writing them down.

*American Indians often drew picture-writing maps on animal hides.*

Some written examples of Indian mapmaking have survived, however. In the early 1500s,

European explorers began coming to the American West. They discovered some Indian maps and saved them. Today these maps are found in libraries and museums. These picture-writing maps describe how an area looked and tell the story of the people who lived there and the events that took place.

Although American Indians once did their picture-writing on tree bark or animal hides, they learned to use paper, pens, and other writing tools after the Europeans arrived. One of the earliest known Indian maps written in pen and ink is called Miguel's Map. Miguel (mi-GEL) was a Pueblo Indian. He was captured by the Spanish and taken to Mexico City, Mexico, probably just after 1600. The Spanish wanted to learn about his homeland in what is now New Mexico. Miguel was told to draw the location of the various Indian villages, also called pueblos. He measured distances between pueblos by counting the number of days it took to get from one to another. Later, Miguel's Map was placed in an archive, a kind of library, in Seville, Spain.

*Although Miguel drew the locations of pueblos on his map, someone else—probably a Spanish official— wrote the words describing them. Since 1602, the Spanish language has changed, so many of the words are different now.*

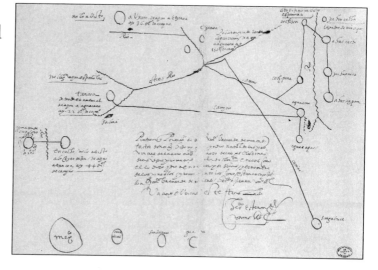

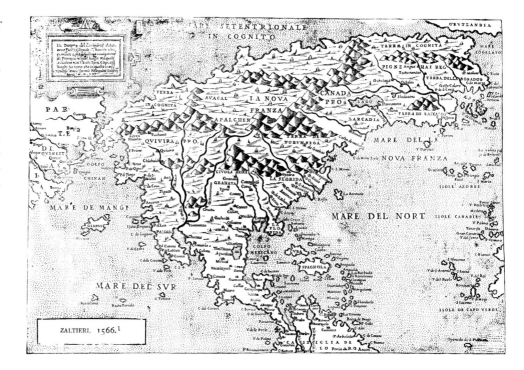

*This 1566 map of North America shows that early maps contained many mistakes. At this time, Europeans mapping the continent did not know its exact shape because it had not been explored fully.*

The Spanish were the first Europeans to explore and map the American West. The Spaniards had maps of North America, but the maps were based on bits and pieces of information and guesswork. So the maps contained many mistakes. For example, many Spanish explorers thought that North America was much smaller than it is.

A Spanish conquistador named Alvar Núñez Cabeza de Vaca was one of the explorers who corrected that mistake. Although others had gone before him, Cabeza de Vaca is generally called the first explorer of the American Southwest. Cabeza de Vaca got there accidentally. In 1527, he left Spain and joined an expedition to Florida. Six hundred people on five ships wanted to explore and claim all the land around the Gulf of Mexico for Spain.

The expedition crossed the Atlantic Ocean and landed in Cuba. In Cuba, the party was pounded by the fiercest storm they had ever seen—a hurricane. A small party went ashore. They fought American Indians, sickness, and hunger, but after the hurricane, Cabeza de Vaca and a few members of his expedition could not find their ships again. Finally, they built five rafts out of logs and sailed west.

*Alvar Núñez Cabeza de Vaca led expeditions in the American Southwest from 1527 to 1537.*

In 1528, they landed at San Luis Island, southwest of what is now Galveston Island, Texas. There, a tribe of American Indians captured Cabeza de Vaca. He managed to escape and began to trade goods with various tribes. He roamed over a large part of the American Southwest. When he saw new places, plants, and animals, he tried to remember them.

After five years as a trader, Cabeza de Vaca was reunited with other survivors of his expedition. Together, they explored what is now New Mexico as far west as the site of El Paso. They met people who were friendly, and some who were not so friendly. More than once, Cabeza de Vaca's party was captured and enslaved. They found evidence—horseshoe nails, buckles, and

*Cabeza de Vaca sailed around the southern coast of what is now the United States. Then he explored parts of present-day Texas, New Mexico, Arizona, and Mexico.*

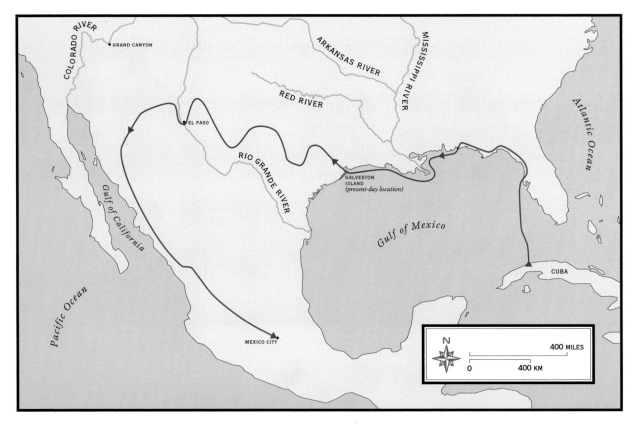

other metal items—that Spaniards had already been in that territory. In 1536, they came upon a party of Spaniards who helped them get to Mexico City, Mexico. There, they were welcomed as conquering heroes.

By August 1537, Cabeza de Vaca was back in Spain. He told the Spanish king about all the new things he had seen—the land formations, the hurricane, and the animals, such as buffalo and possums. He described the food, the houses, and the customs of the Indian peoples. Cabeza de Vaca taught Spaniards much about the American West, and the new information improved their maps of it.

The next major Spanish explorer was Francisco Vásquez de Coronado. He wanted to find the legendary Seven Cities of Gold that supposedly existed somewhere in the American Southwest. In 1539, Coronado sent a priest named Marcos de Niza and an African-American named Estevan to search for the wealthy cities. American Indians told them the first city of gold was Cíbola, to the north. Estevan took a small group ahead to prepare the city for the Spaniards' arrival. Cíbola turned out to be a Zuni pueblo— decorated with turquoise, not gold. Turquoise was of little value. The people of Cíbola warned Estevan to leave, but he refused. After he tried to bribe them with trinkets, they killed his small party. Marcos de Niza hurried back to Coronado.

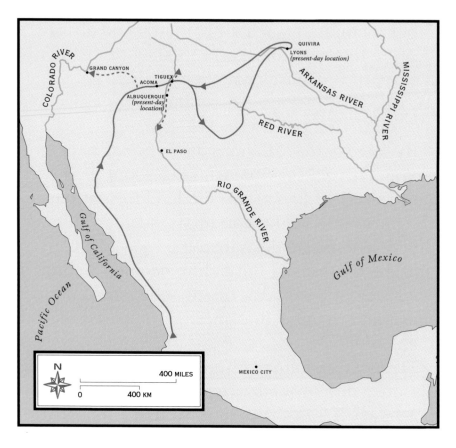

*This map shows the route of Francisco Coronado's expedition in the American Southwest from 1540 to 1542.*

In 1540, Coronado led an expedition from northern Mexico into Arizona and on to New Mexico. Coronado decided that the Seven Cities of Gold must lie to the northwest, so he sent explorers there. They were the first Europeans to see the Grand Canyon of the Colorado River, but they did not find gold.

Coronado had heard of American Indians who lived along the banks of a great river. Searching for the Indians and the river, his expedition came upon a "sky city" called Acoma. The community was a pueblo built on a rock 400 feet

(122 meters) above the ground. Then the party came to Tiguex, on the Rio Grande, just north of present-day Albuquerque, New Mexico. There, the Pueblo Indians welcomed the Europeans. The Pueblo talked about a rich land called Quivira to the north.

Coronado and his party spent the winter in the Rio Grande Valley. Then they marched north and east, looking for Quivira. They came out of New Mexico into what is now northern Texas. The Spaniards called this area *Llano Estacado,* or Staked Plains. The land was big and empty, without landmarks such as trees or hills to guide the expedition. Afraid of being lost in the blinding dust storms, they marked their trail with stakes. They may have named the area accordingly.

*Coronado saw the Rio Grande and the Sandia Mountains when he explored what is now New Mexico.*

Coronado led thirty people north through Texas, across Oklahoma, and into southern Kansas. After thirty days, they came to the Arkansas River Valley. A captain sent out to explore the area returned with a hunting party of Wichita Indians. They said they lived in the valley, which was called Quivira. The Spaniards found no riches there— only one copper ornament worn by a chief. Disappointed, they began to retrace their steps. Near what is now the town of Lyons, Kansas, Coronado raised a wooden marker and claimed all the land for Spain. Then the expedition returned to Mexico.

*This illustration shows Coronado claiming the land he explored for Spain.*

Coronado's journey had lasted more than two years. He and his party had starved, run short of clothing, fought with American Indians, and crossed hot deserts and high mountains. They had not found gold, but Coronado gave the Spanish a better understanding of the enormous size of North America. He proved that the Gulf of Mexico and the Gulf of California did not meet, as many people had thought. He opened trails that later explorers and traders would use to develop the American Southwest. Like Cabeza de Vaca, he provided valuable information about North America. This knowledge was used to make better maps for future explorers and mapmakers.

The Spanish continued to explore. In the 1540s, when Coronado was making his famous expedition, Juan Rodríguez Cabrillo became the first European to see the coast of California. He sailed up the west coast of Mexico, across the Gulf of California, and on to the west coast of California and San Diego Bay. In the 1700s, Gaspar de Portolá led the first land expedition to explore northern California. In 1776, Juan Bautista de Anza led the first Europeans to San Francisco. He is remembered for opening an overland route from San Diego to Monterey. The reports of these Spanish explorers supplied most of the information for maps of the American West until the late 1700s.

*Juan Bautista de Anza*

At this time, the Mississippi River was the United States western boundary. European explorers from the eastern part of North America began to push west. Even with the Spaniards' growing knowledge of the American West, the best maps of it were not very good. Some of the information was wrong. There were wild stories of unusual land formations, such as a mountain of salt. In other instances, mapmakers had to guess. People did not know how high the Rocky Mountains were or where the rivers were west of the Mississippi. They believed the rivers all ran

*This 1798 map of North America shows that explorers and mapmakers still had much to learn about the shape and natural features of the continent. The pink-shaded region is the land that the United States owned at this time.*

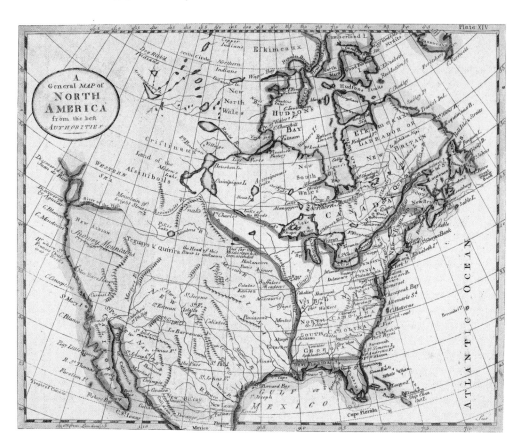

into one another until they reached the Pacific Ocean. Many blanks on maps of the American West needed to be filled in.

Alexander Mackenzie was one of the first British explorers to provide more information for mapmakers. Born in Scotland, Mackenzie moved to New York and then to Canada. In Montreal, Canada, he worked for the North West Company, a fur trading company. In 1789, he took a small party to find a route for traders to the Pacific Ocean—the fabled Northwest Passage. This was supposed to be a waterway across America—continuous and deep enough to carry ships from the Mississippi and Missouri Rivers all the way to the Pacific Ocean. Such a route would have saved traders much transportation time, but Mackenzie's party did not find the Northwest Passage on this trip.

*Alexander Mackenzie*

Mackenzie tried again in 1793, with nine people and a 25-foot (8-m) birchbark canoe. By carrying the canoe across the Continental Divide they managed, after seventy-three days, to float into the Pacific. They had found a Northwest Passage, but it was useless for traders because the rivers that ran east and west did not meet. However, his party was the first expedition to cross North America north of Mexico. In 1801, Mackenzie published a book about his trip called *Voyage from Montreal*.

River travel was very important to traders. The United States wanted to buy land from France to give American traders free use of the Mississippi River and the port of New Orleans. In 1803, the United States bought the Louisiana Territory. This land stretched from the Gulf of Mexico as far north as Canada and from the Mississippi River to the Rocky Mountains. Called the Louisiana Purchase, the land deal nearly doubled the size of the United States by adding 828,000 square miles (2,144,518 square kilometers). The French had called the territory unknown land, but Americans were soon to learn more about it.

*This map shows which countries owned land in North America before the Louisiana Purchase in 1803.*

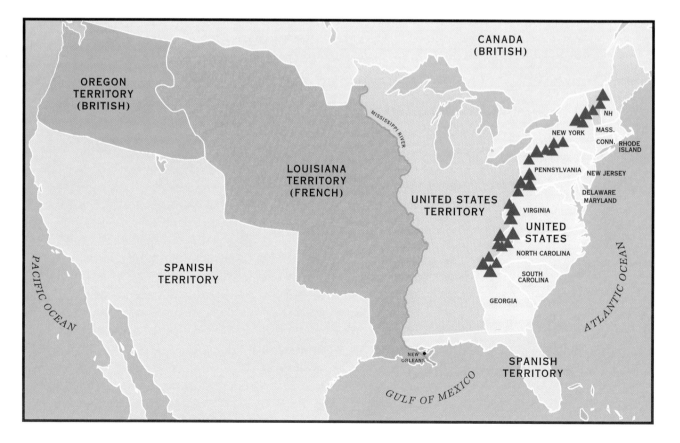

CANADA (BRITISH)

OREGON TERRITORY (BRITISH)

NH

NEW YORK   MASS.

CONN.   RHODE ISLAND

PENNSYLVANIA   NEW JERSEY

LOUISIANA TERRITORY (FRENCH)

DELAWARE MARYLAND

UNITED STATES TERRITORY

VIRGINIA

UNITED STATES

NORTH CAROLINA

SPANISH TERRITORY

SOUTH CAROLINA

GEORGIA

PACIFIC OCEAN

ATLANTIC OCEAN

MISSISSIPPI RIVER

NEW ORLEANS

GULF OF MEXICO

SPANISH TERRITORY

*William Clark (left) and Meriwether Lewis (right)*

President Thomas Jefferson asked his secretary, Captain Meriwether Lewis, to explore the Missouri River and find out whether it connected with the Pacific Ocean. Lewis was a twenty-eight-year-old army officer who knew how to live in the wilderness. He chose William Clark, four years older and "as strong as a bull," as his second-in-command. Their expedition would look for a water route to the Pacific Ocean. On the way, they would study the land, plants, animals, and Indians of the American West.

The Lewis and Clark Expedition is sometimes called the Corps of Discovery. Their journey was one of the most important explorations ever undertaken. To prepare himself, Lewis studied many subjects and read Mackenzie's book, *Voyage from Montreal.* Lewis packed clothing, tools, scientific books, medicine, rifles, and trade goods. He also bought a huge black dog—a Newfoundland that he called Seamen.

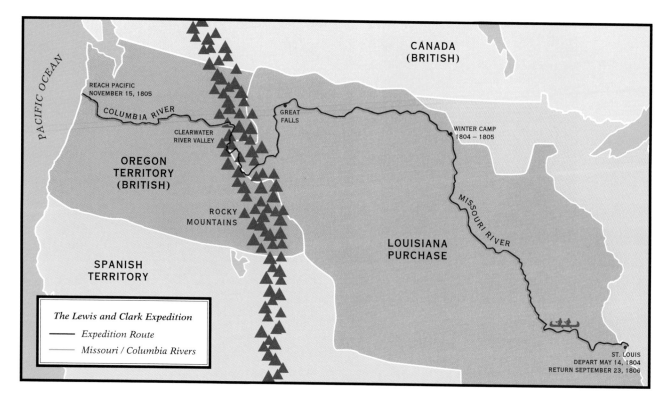

*This map shows the route of the Lewis and Clark Expedition from 1804 to 1806.*

The expedition started up the Missouri River on May 14, 1804. They soon began to see animals that were new to them—pronghorn antelope, buffalo, prairie dogs, jackrabbits, and coyotes. They also suffered from mosquitoes, gnats, and ticks. The expedition met American Indians—the Hidatsa and Mandan, the Otoe and Missouri, the threatening Teton Sioux and the friendly Yankton Sioux, and the Arikara.

Lewis and Clark made their winter camp in present-day North Dakota among the Mandan Indians. The Mandan leader, Chief Big White, drew rough maps in sand of the Upper Missouri River and its connecting streams. Chief Big White

and maps given to him by American Indians. He measured and described what he saw, and he drew pictures of the land and water. He named rivers, meadows, mountain passes, and rock formations. Many of those names have changed, but some are still called by the names Clark gave them. His sketches and the dozens of notebooks he filled were the basis for the first official map of the American Northwest. This map was published in 1814. Maps began to look more like those we use today after the Lewis and Clark Expedition.

*Clark's map of the Great Falls of the Missouri names places, measures distances, and shows the slope of the falls.*

21

*Zebulon Pike*

*Pikes Peak is the snowcapped mountain behind the red sandstone rock formation. The mountain named after Zebulon Pike is near Colorado Springs, Colorado.*

Zebulon Montgomery Pike was another important explorer of the early 1800s. In 1805, Pike was directed to find the source of the Mississippi River and "calculate distances by time, noting rivers, creeks, Highland, prairies, islands, rapids, shoals, mines, Quarries, Timber, water, Soil, Indian Villages and Settlements, in a Diary." He was also to get permission from the American Indians for the government to build forts. Pike and his party thought that Red Cedar Lake (now Cass Lake) and Leech Lake in northern Minnesota were the source of the Mississippi River. Later expeditions found the real source, Lake Itasca, farther north and east—but still in Minnesota.

In July 1806, Pike was sent to explore the Arkansas and Red Rivers. His party arrived at the eastern slope of the Rocky Mountains in what is now Colorado. There, Pike called one towering mountain "Grand Peak." Today this mountain is known as Pikes Peak, and it stands 14,110 feet (4301 m) high. Pike and his expedition tried to climb the mountain, but they did not succeed.

From the Arkansas River, Pike's party headed south. The Spaniards, protective of their land, promptly arrested Pike's group for illegally entering the area. Pike was treated well and released in 1807, but the Spaniards kept all his notes and papers. As a result, Pike had no written record of the route his party had taken or the things they had seen.

During the 1800s, the U.S. Army made many important contributions to maps of the West. Beginning in 1802, army engineers were trained in mapmaking at the United States Military Academy at West Point. By 1813, the army was conducting surveys to plan routes for troops.

One army engineer, Major Stephen H. Long, led an 1819 expedition to explore the Rocky Mountains. Long said that the land in what is now Colorado was not fit for settlement. On the official map of his route, he marked the Great Plains as the "Great Desert." His opinion about this region convinced many people not to settle there for almost forty years. Most easterners thought that the American West was a wild, deserted place in which no one could live.

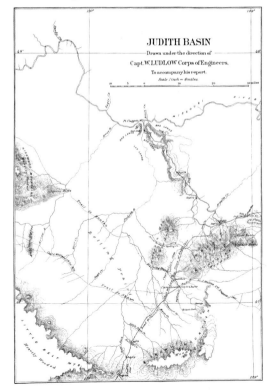

*In 1875, a U.S. Army engineer drew this map of Judith Basin, in central Montana. The mapmaker used curved lines to illustrate the shape of the mountains and dotted lines to mark trails.*

*John C. Frémont*

*Jessie Benton
Frémont*

Another member of the U.S. Army, John C. Frémont, changed many people's opinions about the American West. Frémont served on the U.S. Army Topographical Corps' first major western project—an 1839 expedition into the land between the upper Mississippi and Missouri Rivers. He served under the French explorer Joseph Nicolas Nicolett, who taught him the art of mapmaking. After the expedition, Frémont married Jessie Benton, the daughter of Senator Thomas Hart Benton of Missouri.

Benton believed that all land between the Atlantic and Pacific Oceans should belong to the United States. He persuaded Congress to sponsor surveys of the Oregon Trail in 1842, the Oregon Territory in 1844, and California in 1845. Benton made sure that his son-in-law led these expeditions. Frémont was ordered to survey and map the land. In addition, he was to write descriptions that would persuade Americans to travel and settle in the West. Frémont was only a fair mapmaker and surveyor, but his vivid descriptions of the land he had seen became popular with the public. His wife, Jessie, helped him write them. Frémont's work helped encourage settlement of the American West.

Even though the army engineers knew a lot about mapping, they still made mistakes. Some mapping errors were found in the mid-1800s, when the Mexican War (1846–1848) ended. In part, the United States fought this war to get more land.

Under the 1848 Treaty of Guadalupe Hidalgo (gwahd-uhl-OOP hih-DAHL-goh), Mexico surrendered land that became the states of California, Nevada, Utah, and parts of Colorado, Arizona, New Mexico, and Wyoming. Maps were needed to mark the new boundaries between Mexico and the United States.

Mapmaker William H. Emory of the U.S. Army Topographical Corps started mapping the area in 1844—before the war—using information from an earlier map. This information had the Rio Grande River and the city of El Paso del Norte in the wrong places. The errors caused difficulties in treaty terms. After the war, Emory served on the Mexican Boundary Survey that corrected these errors and fixed the new borders.

*This man is looking through a sextant, an instrument sometimes used by mapmakers to measure distances.*

An accurate map tells the position of a place by two lines—lines of longitude that run from north to south and lines of latitude that run from east to west. By the 1840s, mapmakers had equipment that helped them locate places and measure distances along these lines. Most expeditions carried instruments that allowed them to measure angles, distances, and heights. Astronomical tables and other information were also available. The new equipment helped mapmaking become more exact.

Railroad companies needed accurate maps to find the best places to put down their railroad tracks. There were many railroad lines east of the Mississippi River by 1850. That year, the U.S. Congress began discussing the possibility of a transcontinental railroad that would stretch from the Atlantic Ocean to the Pacific Ocean. In 1853, Army engineers and surveyors began exploring for possible routes for the transcontinental railroad. They noted where the land was level and suitable for tracks and where it was not. These railroad surveys filled in many blank spaces on maps of the American West. By the late 1800s, almost every river and mountain of any importance appeared on U.S. government maps and had been given a name.

*This drawing shows people working on the railroad in the American West. Without maps, people could not build railroads.*

In 1879, the U.S. Geological Survey, a government organization that had been surveying the American West to learn more about its soil, rock, and minerals, officially began mapping the country. Since the U.S. Geological Survey began its work, mapmaking has changed a great deal.

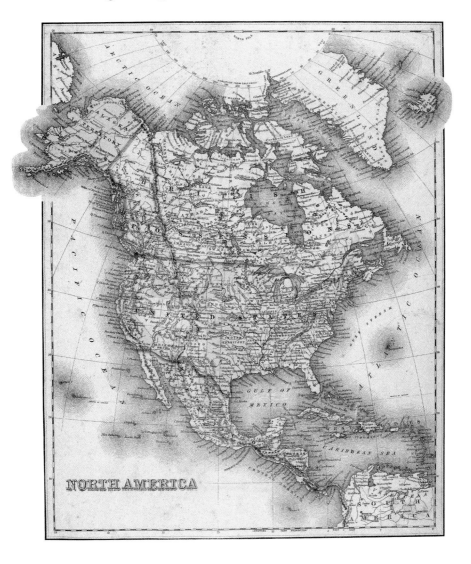

*This 1875 map of North America looks similar to maps of today. Can you name the states and countries that were not formed at this time?*

Today, there are all kinds of maps—maps for hikers, maps for scientists, maps of vegetation, maps of highways, and maps that show how many people live in a particular area. Political maps illustrate the boundaries that mark cities, counties, states, or countries. Shaded relief maps show the shape and features of the land—mountains, valleys, rivers, and lakes. Topographic maps use imaginary lines and different colors to show how high an area is above sea level. Most mapmakers now create maps on computers. Information technology continues to improve the process of mapping and its accuracy.

*Vegetation maps show what types of plants grow in an area. This vegetation map of the United States was created in 1926, so the information may have changed since then.*

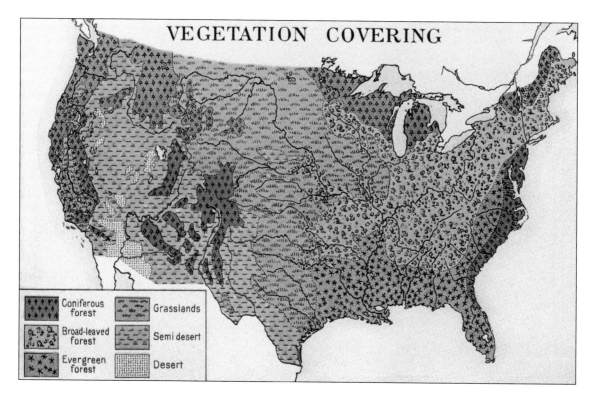

VEGETATION COVERING

Coniferous forest

Broad-leaved forest

Evergreen forest

Grasslands

Semi desert

Desert

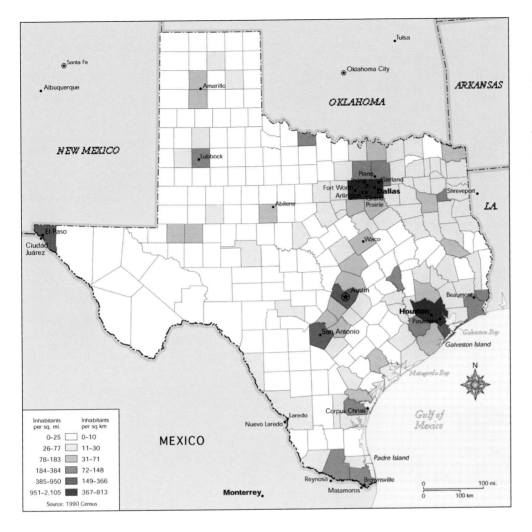

Inhabitants per sq. mi. | Inhabitants per sq km
---|---
0–25 | 0–10
26–77 | 11–30
78–183 | 31–71
184–384 | 72–148
385–950 | 149–366
951–2,105 | 367–813

Source: 1990 Census

*Population maps show the number of people who live in an area. This population map shows that more Texans live in or near cities.*

Although the methods of mapmaking have changed, the purpose of mapmaking has remained the same through the years. People still collect, organize, and express new information about places so that others can learn more about them by reading a map. Modern knowledge about the American West would not be as great without the early maps of the American Indians, explorers, military, railroad companies, and the U.S. government.

# GLOSSARY

**archive** – a place where historical documents are kept

**boundary** – a line or limit marking the end of something, such as a city or a country

**conquistador** – a leader of the Spanish conquest of Mexico, the American Southwest, and Peru in the 1500s

**Continental Divide** – an elevated area in the Rocky Mountains that separates rivers that flow west from rivers that flow east

**document** – a paper that provides information or proof

**engineer** – a person who designs and builds things, such as bridges, roads, or tunnels

**expedition** – a journey made for a definite purpose or the group making such a journey

**Great Plains** – vast dry grasslands in North America that extend from northern Canada to Texas

**Louisiana Purchase** – land the United States purchased from France in 1803 for $15 million

**petroglyph** – a carving or message on a rock

**prehistoric** – the time before people recorded history in writing

**pueblo** – a village of buildings made of adobe or stone usually built by Indians of the American Southwest

**route** – a specific road or line of travel

**survey** – (verb) to find out measurements, position, boundaries, or elevation of a land by measuring angles and distances; (noun) the act of measuring land

**topographical** – relating to maps and landscape

**turquoise** – a greenish-blue semi-precious stone

*Zebulon Pike led an expedition to search for the source of the Mississippi River.*

*Map Rock is a famous petroglyph.*

# TIMELINE

**1528** Cabeza de Vaca lands at Galveston Island, Texas

Francisco Coronado's expedition searches for Seven Cities of Gold

{ **1540**
**1541**

**1602** Miguel's Map

**1776** Juan Bautista de Anza leads Europeans to San Francisco

**1789**

Alexander Mackenzie tries to find Northwest Passage

**1793** Mackenzie finds water route, but large ships cannot travel on it

**1803** Louisiana Purchase

**1804**
**1806** } Lewis and Clark Expedition; Pike Expedition

**1814** First official map of Lewis and Clark Expedition published

Major Stephen H. Long reports that Great Plains are not fit to live in **1819**

**1839**

John C. Frémont's first expedition to upper Missouri and Mississippi Rivers

**1842** Frémont's expedition to Oregon Trail

William Emory's faulty map of Texas-Mexico boundary; Frémont's expedition to Oregon Territory

**1844**
**1845** Frémont's expedition to California

**1846**
**1848** } Mexican War

**1879** U.S. Geological Survey begins officially mapping United States

# INDEX

## PHOTO CREDITS

Photographs ©: American Philosophical Society Library, Philadelphia: 21; Art Resource, NY: 24 top (National Portrait Gallery, Smithsonian Institution); Bridgeman Art Library International Ltd., London/New York: 28 (BAL126338/Map showing the vegetation covering the United States of America, from 'The Pagent of America, Vol. 3', by Ralph Henry Gabriel, 1926, lithograph, Private Collection); Corbis-Bettmann: 22 bottom (David Muench), 6, 12, 13, 24 bottom, 26; Givens Hot Springs: 3, 30 bottom (Nadine Givens); Ministerio de Educación y Cultura Archivo General de Indias: 5, 31 right; Montana Historical Society, Helena: cover, detail of "Lewis and Clark at Three Forks", by E. S. Paxson. Mural at Montana State Capitol, 19 (Don Beatty); North Wind Picture Archives: 4, 7, 11, 22 top, 25, 30 top; Stock Montage, Inc.: 1, 15, 31 left (The Newberry Library), 2, 14, 17, 27; US Army Corps of Engineers: 23; XNR Productions, Inc.: 29.

Maps by TJS Design, Inc.

## PICTURE IDENTIFICATIONS

Cover: This section of a painting shows the Lewis and Clark Expedition at what is now Three Forks, Montana.

Page 1: A mapmaker drew this beautiful hand-drawn map of the world in 1630.

Page 2: Explorers and mapmakers of the American West often had to walk and climb steep mountains.

## ABOUT THE AUTHOR

Judy Alter has lived in the American West for more than thirty years and studied its history and geography. She is director of Texas Christian University Press. Her writing about the West has won several awards from Western Writers of America and the National Cowboy Hall of Fame.